MATHS MAGIC

Multiplying and Dividing

Written by Wendy Clemson
and David Clemson

TWO CAN

LONDON ■ PRINCETON

www.two-canpublishing.com

Published by Two-Can Publishing
43-45 Dorset Street, London W1U 7NA

www.two-canpublishing.com

© Two-Can Publishing 2002

For information on Two-Can books and multimedia,
call (0)20 7224 2440, fax (0)20 7224 7005
or visit our website at http://www.two-canpublishing.com

Created by
act-two
346 Old Street
London EC1V 9RB

www.act-two.com

Authors: Wendy Clemson and David Clemson

Editor: Penny Smith
Designers: Maggi Howells and Helen Holmes
Illustrators: Andy Peters and Mike Stones
Photographer: Daniel Pangbourne
Pre-press production: Adam Wilde

'Two-Can' is a trademark of Two-Can Publishing.
Two-Can Publishing is a division of Zenith Entertainment plc,
43-45 Dorset Street, London W1U 7NA

Hardback ISBN 1-85434-878-7
Paperback ISBN 1-85434-879-5

Dewey Decimal Classification 513

Hardback 10 9 8 7 6 5 4 3 2 1
Paperback 10 9 8 7 6 5 4 3 2 1

A catalogue record for this book is available
from the British Library.

Colour reproduction by Colourscan Overseas, Singapore
Printed by Printing Express in Hong Kong

Contents

Multiply or divide?

This book is all about multiplying and dividing. Multiplying is a quick way of adding the same number to itself over and over. Dividing is a way of sharing things out equally. In our farmyard, the animals have fun questions for you. Can you work out the answers? Do you need to multiply or divide?

1. There are three hens in the farmyard and they've laid two eggs each. How many eggs have they laid altogether?

2. There are two big cats and eight kittens. Each big cat has the same number of kittens. How many kittens does each big cat have?

Counting in pairs

Take a look at the animals standing in pairs along the trail. How many are there altogether? The quickest way to find the answer is to count them two by two. This is the same as multiplying. Use the big stack of rocks to help you.

1 Start at the beginning of the trail and count all the pairs of animals behind the pile of rocks. Check your answer below.

2 Now how many animals can you count between the rocks and the cactus?

When you count in twos, you're using the two times table.

The rock stack numbers:
24, 22, 20, 18, 16, 14, 12, 10, 8, 6, 4, 2

cactus

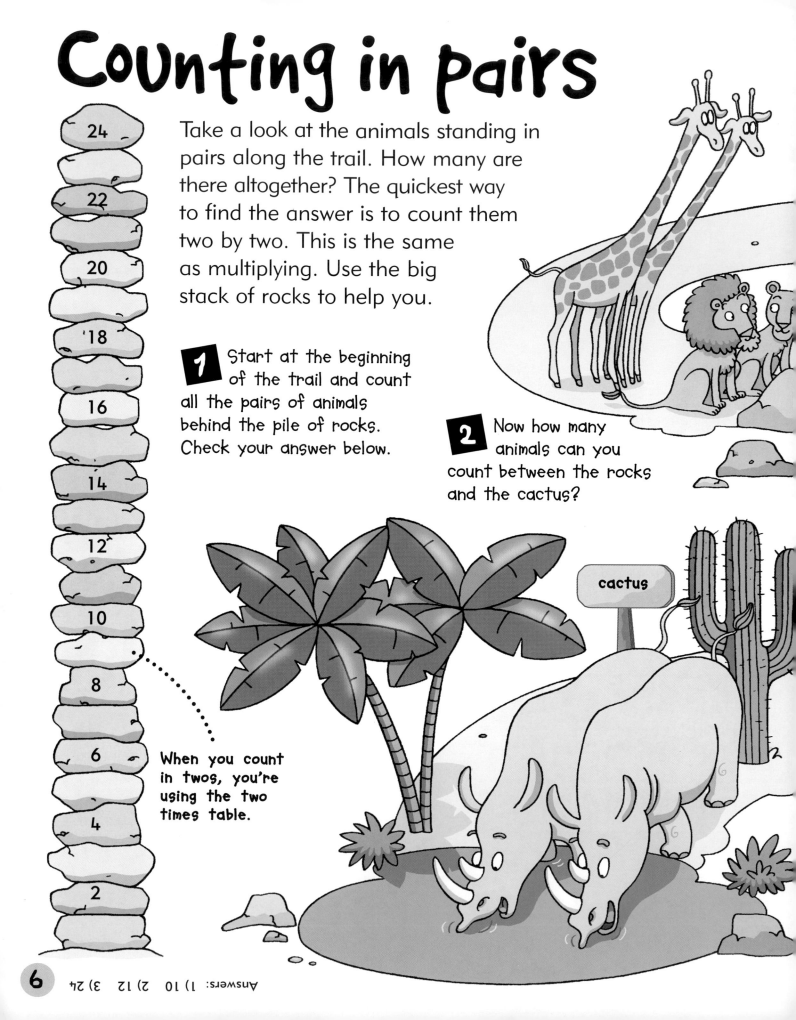

START

pile of rocks

3 What's the total number of animals in this picture? Count the pairs to see.

Now try this

BRAIN teaser

Challenge a friend to count in twos up to 24. 2, 4, 6.... Look at the stack of rocks on the opposite page to check if he's right. Now, can he answer these questions?

What comes before 16?

14

What comes after 10?

12

What comes on either side of 6?

4 and 8

PROVE IT!

Count the toys in the picture. There are twelve, two of each kind. Now put the toys into groups of two, so you have two balls, two boats and so on. Do you have fewer groups than toys? Yes! You have six groups – that's half the number of toys.

7

Counting in groups

If you group things together they are much easier to count. Try this. Scatter a handful of marbles over the floor and look at them quickly. How many are there? Now arrange the marbles in neat lines. Are the marbles easier to count?

Make bug cards

YOU WILL NEED
ruler, felt pens, card, eggcup, scissors

Making rows and columns

An array is an arrangement of rows and columns. Here, you can see how to make six marbles into two oblong-shaped arrays.

A row runs from side to side.

This array has three rows of two marbles and two columns of three marbles.

A column runs up and down.

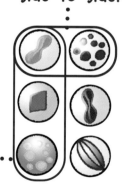

This array has two rows of three marbles and three columns of two marbles.

1 First use a ruler to draw a grid of 20 squares. The squares should have sides of about 7 cm each.

2 Draw around an eggcup to make a circle in the middle of each square. Decorate the circles to look like bugs.

3 Cut out each square and you'll have 20 bug cards. Now see what you can do with them!

8

4 You can make each of the numbers 6, 8, 10, 14, 15 and 18 into two oblong-shaped arrays. Use your bug cards to work out what these arrays look like.

5 You can make the number 20 into four oblong-shaped arrays. Try making these arrays with your bug cards too.

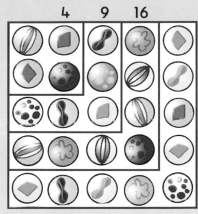

Top tip

Some numbers cannot be made into oblong-shaped arrays. The number 7 is a good example. Look at the picture to see how it works.

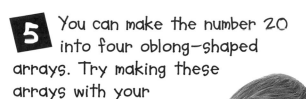

This array has two rows of four bugs and four columns of two bugs.

Apple pickers

Here's a fruity game to help you master multiplication. To play it, you'll need to use the two, three, four and five times tables. If you need help with these, take a look at the multiplication square on page 31.

Make the spinner and cards

YOU WILL NEED

tracing paper, pencil, ruler, card, felt pen, scissors, cocktail stick, paper

1 First trace this spinner on to a piece of card. Copy the numbers and cut out the spinner. Push the cocktail stick through the middle so you can twirl the spinner around.

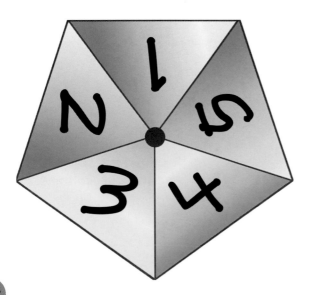

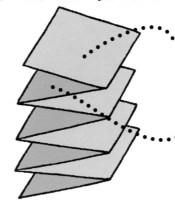

THE MULTIPLICATION SIGN

Look at this calculation $4 \times 2 = 8$

The $\times$ sign means multiply by. So here you multiply 4 by 2 to get 8.

Another way of saying this is 4 times 2 equals 8.

2 Now cut out a long strip of paper and fold it to make a concertina of squares like the one shown here.

First fold over a square of paper at one end of the strip.

Then fold the strip backwards and forwards to make a concertina of squares.

3 Draw an apple on the top square. Cut round the apple through all the squares to make several apples at once. You need 40 apples, so you may need to fold up a few strips of paper. Write these numbers on the apples:

2	2	3	3	4
4	4	4	5	5
6	6	6	6	8
8	8	8	9	9
10	10	10	10	12
12	12	12	15	15
15	15	16	16	20
20	20	20	25	25

Now try this

BRAIN teaser

Challenge a friend to put these numbers and signs in the right order to make multiplications that work.

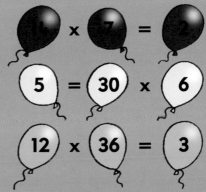

Here are the answers.
1) 2 x 7 = 14 and 7 x 2 = 14
2) 5 x 6 = 30 and 6 x 5 = 30
3) 3 x 12 = 36 and 12 x 3 = 36

4 Now play the game with a friend. Spread the cards out on the table. Each choose one number from below.

| 2 | 3 | 4 | 5 |

5 Take turns to spin the spinner, then multiply the number that comes up by the number you have chosen. Is your answer on one of the apples? If it is, keep that apple. The first person to pick up 10 apples is the winner.

2 x 4 = 8. Hurray! I can pick up an apple with the number 8.

11

Fives and tens

Knowing how to count quickly in fives and tens is extremely useful. It helps you to count money or even to play the space race game here. Use the five and ten times tables below to see if you can be the first to reach Planet Zorro!

HOW TO PLAY

◆ This is a game for two to four earthling players. Take turns to throw one dice. Move forwards the number of places shown on the dice.

◆ When you land on a 5 or 10, throw the dice again. Multiply the 5 or 10 by the number on the dice. Move your counter to the next square with this answer.

◆ When you land on a black hole, go wherever it takes you.

◆ The first to finish is the winner. To land there, you must throw exactly the number you need. Until you do, you're stuck!

Counting cosmic cash

How quickly can you answer these testing questions on cosmic coins? Look at the picture to see.

1 How many 5 Zorros coins are worth the same as a 10 Zorros coin?

2 How many 10 Zorros coins are worth the same as a 50 Zorros coin? Check your answer below.

3 How many 50 Zorros coins are worth the same as 100 Zorros? Look below to check.

FIVE AND TEN TIMES TABLES

5 times table	10 times table
1 x 5 = 5	1 x 10 = 10
2 x 5 = 10	2 x 10 = 20
3 x 5 = 15	3 x 10 = 30
4 x 5 = 20	4 x 10 = 40
5 x 5 = 25	5 x 10 = 50
6 x 5 = 30	6 x 10 = 60
7 x 5 = 35	7 x 10 = 70
8 x 5 = 40	8 x 10 = 80
9 x 5 = 45	9 x 10 = 90
10 x 5 = 50	10 x 10 = 100
11 x 5 = 55	11 x 10 = 110
12 x 5 = 60	12 x 10 = 120

Sailing game

All aboard! In this great sailing game you'll see how three numbers can be multiplied in any order to reach the same answer. Look at the playing boards. On each one the same numbers are used, but in different orders. Can you work out the missing numbers?

Make the sailboard game

YOU WILL NEED
scissors, coloured paper,
ruler, coloured card,
glue, felt pens or paints

1 First make 36 yellow sails. Cut several long strips of yellow paper about 7 cm wide. Fold them as shown, then cut triangles through all the layers. Now, make 15 orange sails for answer cards.

2 For the playing boards, cut out four oblongs of blue card. Make sure they are big enough to fit 12 boats each. Glue your yellow sails on the boards as shown. Then paint the rest of each boat. Copy the numbers.

playing boards

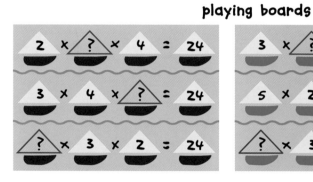
$2 \times ? \times 4 = 24$
$3 \times 4 \times ? = 24$
$? \times 3 \times 2 = 24$

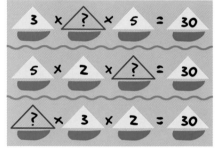
$3 \times ? \times 5 = 30$
$5 \times 2 \times ? = 30$
$? \times 3 \times 2 = 30$

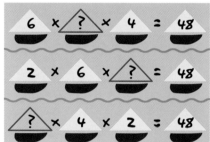
$6 \times ? \times 4 = 48$
$2 \times 6 \times ? = 48$
$? \times 4 \times 2 = 48$

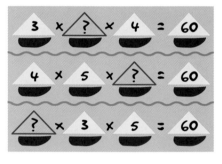
$3 \times ? \times 4 = 60$
$4 \times 5 \times ? = 60$
$? \times 3 \times 5 = 60$

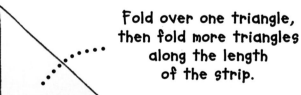

Fold over one triangle, then fold more triangles along the length of the strip.

cut here

3 Now finish off your orange answer cards by copying these numbers on to them.

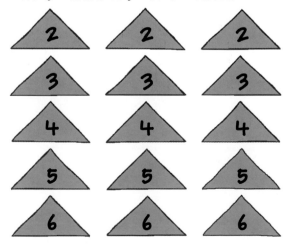

HOW TO PLAY

◆ This game is for two players. Each player takes two playing boards.

◆ Shuffle the orange answer cards and put them in a pile, face down. Take turns to pick up the top card. If an answer card completes a calculation on one of your playing boards, put it on that board. If it doesn't, put the answer card face down on a separate pile.

◆ When you have finished taking cards from the first answer card pile, work your way through the used answer cards. The first person to fill in two boards is the winner.

3 x 4 x 2 = 24.
Hurray!

Use both playing boards at the same time.

pile of answer cards

Missing numbers

This is a page for number detectives. It's full of tricky number mysteries for you to solve. The problem is that only part of the information is here. Your job is to work out what's missing by looking closely at the numbers on the page. Are you clued-up enough to answer the questions?

Top tip

There are different ways to say 'multiply by two'. As well as the phrase above, you can say 'make that twice as much' or 'double your number'.

Find the missing jewels

A hidden route along the street leads you to the house with the jewels. Follow it by finding the number that's missing from each calculation. This number tells you which house to visit.

Start with the clue in the detective's hand. Then follow the trail until you reach number 50 – that's where the jewels are hidden. And don't leave the trail or you'll go nowhere!

FIRST CLUE
2 x ? = 20
The missing number tells you which house to visit.

Go to
1 x ? = 2

Go to
1 x 11 = ?

Go to
? x 2 = 12

Go to
? x 6 = 30

Go to
4 x ? = 12

Go to
3 x 3 = ?

Go to
? x 27 = 27

Work out the answers

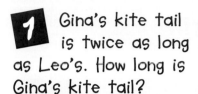

Leo   Gina

1 Gina's kite tail is twice as long as Leo's. How long is Gina's kite tail?

2 Leo's rocket is three times as tall as Gina's. How tall is his rocket?

3 Gina has five times more swap cards than Leo. How many does she have?

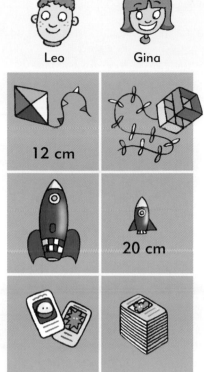

12 cm

20 cm

Answers: 1) 24 cm   2) 60 cm   3) 10 swap cards

BRAIN teaser

Look at the three times table below. Challenge a friend to add together each of the double digits. What are the answers? Is there a pattern?

1 x 3 = 3	**These are double digits.**
2 x 3 = 6	
3 x 3 = 9	
4 x 3 = 12	(1 + 2)
5 x 3 = 15	(1 + 5)
6 x 3 = 18	(1 + 8)
7 x 3 = 21	(2 + 1)
8 x 3 = 24	(2 + 4)
9 x 3 = 27	(2 + 7)
10 x 3 = 30	(3 + 0)

The answers are always 3, 6, 9, 3, 6, 9, 3, 6, 9.

8

10

12

14

Go to 13 x 1 = ?

Go to ? x 4 = 16

Go to 2 x ? = 24

Go to 3 x 5 =?

Go to 2 x ? =16

Go to 2 x 7 = ?

Go to 5 x 10 = ?

Go to 1 x ? = 7

9

11

13

15

Answer: You visit houses in this order 10, 4, 11, 15, 7, 1, 5, 9, 8, 13. The jewels are hidden at house number 13.

fair shares

How often do you share sweets or toys with your friends? Each time you do, you are dividing. But to be good at dividing you have to practise. So start by looking at the creepy-crawlies in the big picture. Can you see how many ways they can be shared?

Share and share alike

1 Look at the big group of creepy-crawlies. How many are there? Now imagine sharing them equally between two people. How many will each person have? Count the creepy-crawlies in the picture below to check your answer.

How many have you got?

2 If the creepy-crawlies are put into five piles, how many will there be in each pile? Count to check.

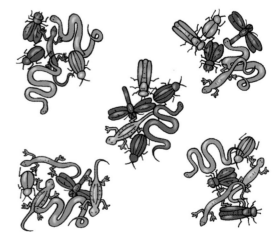

3 Three people want equal shares of the creepy-crawlies. How many can each person have? Count the platefuls to check your answer.

4 If ten people each take one creepy-crawly from the pile, how many more creepy-crawlies can they each take? Look at the picture below to help you.

PROVE IT!

One way to share things out is to take away the same number again and again. You can prove it with this number track.

Let's say you want to share 16 toys between two friends. First place your finger on the number of toys.

Now jump back two places at a time until you reach zero. You make eight jumps, so two friends have eight toys each!

0 - 1 - 2 - 3 - 4 - 5 - 6 - 7 - 8 - 9 - 10 - 11 - 12 - 13 - 14 - 15 - 16 - 17 - 18 - 19 - 20

8   7   6   5   4   3   2   1

Jump back in twos because there are two people sharing.

This is the number of toys.

A slice of cake

Here's a quick quiz. You have six little cakes to divide between three people. How many cakes can each person have? The answer is two cakes each. You can also divide a whole cake. But to do this, you have to cut it up into slices. Each slice is a fraction of the whole cake. Use your cake slices to play the party cake game below!

Make the slices of cake

YOU WILL NEED
felt pens, coloured paper, small plate, scissors

1 First prepare your cakes. Draw around a small plate to make 12 paper circles. Decorate each circle to make four of each of the cakes shown here.

chocolate cake

lemon cake

strawberry cake

THE DIVISION SIGN

÷ This sign means divide.

So when you talk about the calculation

$8 \div 2 = 4$

you say eight divided by two equals four.

2 Fold each chocolate cake exactly in half. Then cut along the folds. You will have eight chocolate slices.

Divide each chocolate cake into two equal slices.

3 Fold your strawberry cakes in half, then half again. Cut along the folds. You will have 16 strawberry slices.

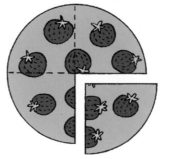

Divide each strawberry cake into four equal slices.

4 Fold each lemon cake in half. Fold it in half again and then again to make eight slices. Then cut them out. You will have 32 lemon slices.

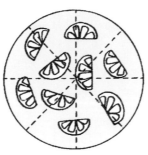

Divide each lemon cake into eight equal slices.

5 Now play the game. Mix up the slices and share them with a friend. You'll each have 28 slices. How many whole cakes can you make up from a mixture of slices? Whoever makes the most cakes is the winner.

Make your cakes from different-sized slices.

Top tip

When you divide an object into two equal pieces, the pieces are called halves. Four equal pieces are called quarters. Eight equal pieces are called eighths.

halves   quarters   eighths

PROVE IT!

You can write fractions using numbers. Take a look at the divided-up cakes here to see how to do it.

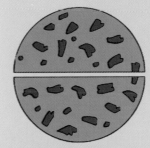

This cake is made up of 2 slices. Each slice is 1 of 2. You can write this as $\frac{1}{2}$.

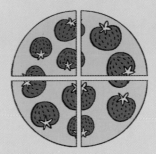

There are 4 slices that make up the whole cake here. Each slice is 1 of 4 so you write this as $\frac{1}{4}$.

Count the slices on this cake. You'll see there are 8. Each slice is $\frac{1}{8}$ of the whole cake.

Mix and match

The truly magical thing about multiplying and dividing is that you can turn one into the other, simply by changing the order of the numbers! So the calculation 4 x 2 = 8 can turn into 8 ÷ 2 = 4. Play the mix and match game here to see if you can both multiply and divide the numbers on your cards.

play cards

Make the mix and match cards

YOU WILL NEED
coloured card, ruler, felt pens, scissors

1 First make sign cards by drawing six squares on a piece of card and copying the signs shown here. Cut out the cards.

sign cards

2 Now make your play cards. Draw a grid of 14 squares and copy the numbers in this picture on to it. Cut out the squares.

3 Then make your pick-up cards. Draw 28 squares, copy on the numbers below and cut out the squares.

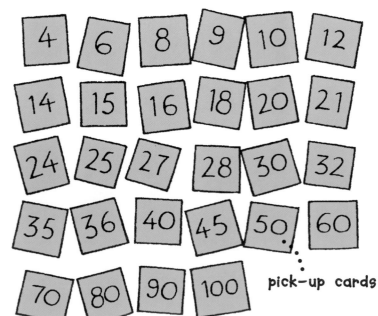

pick-up cards

22

HOW TO PLAY

◆ This is a game for you and one friend. Take three different sign cards each. Then shuffle the play cards and share them equally between you. Put the pick-up cards in a pile face down on the table.

◆ Lay your play cards out in front of you. Then take turns to collect a pick-up card. Can you make a multiplication or division with the pick-up card and your play and sign cards? If you can, keep the pick-up card. If you can't, take it out of the game.

◆ The game ends when you have used up all the pick-up cards. Whoever has collected the most pick-up cards is the winner.

PROVE IT!

You can turn a multiplication sum into a division because multiplying is the inverse, or opposite, of dividing. Look at the calculations to see how the signs change but the numbers stay the same.

$$10 \div 5 = 2$$

$$2 \times 5 = 10$$

You can multiply or divide your numbers.

I've picked up number 20. I can use 2 and 10 from my play cards to make a calculation.

sign cards

pick-up cards

play cards

23

Doubling and halving

Multiplying by two is called doubling and dividing by two is called halving. Most snakes on this page are double or half the length of each other. But which is which? To find out, check the measurements of all the snakes, then answer the questions.

Which snake is which?

YOU WILL NEED
string, felt-tip pen, ruler

1 Check each snake's length by laying the end of the string on the snake's nose and the rest along its body. Mark the string where it touches the tip of the tail. Then measure the string with a ruler.

2 Now work out which colour snake is double the length of the red snake.

3 Look at the measurements again. Which snake is half the length of the purple snake?

4 Which snake is twice the length of the green snake?

5 Which snake is half the total length of the pink and orange snakes?

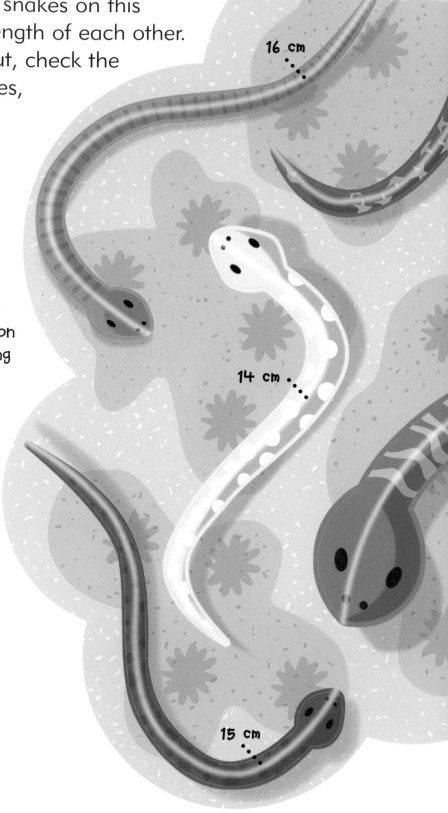

16 cm

14 cm

15 cm

Answers: 2) blue snake 3) orange snake 4) pink snake 5) yellow snake

24 cm

12 cm

30 cm

8 cm

Now try this

BRAIN teaser

Think of a number

3

Double it.

6

Add 20.

26

Halve it.

13

Take away 9.

4

Take away your starting number.
The answer is 1.

1

Think of another number.
What happens this time?

Top tip

You can use a thin strip of paper, a pipe-cleaner or thick cotton thread to measure the snakes. Write down your measurements in centimetres.

Measure each snake from the tip of its nose to the tip of its tail.

Remainders

Have you ever tried sharing things equally between your friends, and ended up with some left over? This leftover is called the remainder. It's useful to know about remainders because they can help you to solve all kinds of problems in everyday life, such as the questions on the opposite page.

such as the questions on the opposite page.

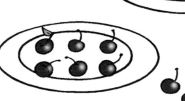

Top Tip

You always have a remainder when you divide an odd number by an even number. Here, five cherries are divided by two. There is one cherry left over.

First look at remainders

YOU WILL NEED
4 paper plates, 20 cherries

1 Lay out four paper plates and share the 20 cherries between them. You won't have any remainders because 20 can be divided exactly by 4.

One for you... and one for you...

2 Now try sharing 20 cherries between three plates. You'll see that this division doesn't work out exactly. Look at the picture below to check the remainder.

3 This time just use 17 of the cherries and share them between two plates. Try to imagine the answer before you check the picture below.

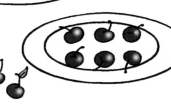

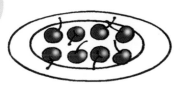
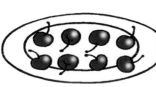

Birthday surprise!

Answer these birthday questions to work out the remainders.

1 You've got 25 minutes before you leave for your special day. You take 10 minutes to open your cards, then 10 minutes to open your presents. Do you have any time left over?

2 Next you go shopping. You've been given £20.00 as a special treat. You buy four toys at £3.00 each. How much money is left?

3 Finally, you and your friends meet at the fair. There are two cars on the big dipper, each with eight seats. But 20 people want to get on. How many will have to wait for the next ride?

PROVE IT!

These two cards are the remainder.

If you share five cards between you and two friends and you keep the remainder, you will have three times as many cards as them.

If, instead of keeping the remainder, you share it between your friends, they will each have twice as many cards as you!

Your friends have two cards each. You have one card.

Answers: 1) 5 minutes left over. 2) £8.00 left 3) 4 people

True or false?

This puzzling page is full of quick tips for multiplying and dividing. But which facts are true and which are false? Work out the answers, then check your score on the rainbow.

1 Every answer in the ten times table ends in 0.
True or false?

$1 \times 10 = 10$

$3 \times 10 = 30$

$5 \times 10 = 50$

4 If you divide a cake into 8 equal slices, 4 people can have 2 slices each or 2 people can have 4 slices each.
True or false?

$8 \div 2 = 4$

$8 \div 4 = 2$

2 Seven can be divided exactly only by the numbers one and seven.
True or false?

$7 \div 1 = 7$

5 Any number that ends in two can be divided by two.
True or false?

$12 \div 2 = 6$

$32 \div 2 = 16$

3 When you multiply, the answer is always smaller than the numbers you started with.
True or false?

$10 \times 7 = 70$ $6 \times 5 = 30$

6 Multiplying is the same as adding a number to itself over and over again.
True or false?

$3 \times 2 = 6$ $2 + 2 + 2 = 6$

7 All odd numbers, such as 3 and 7, can be divided exactly by two.
True or false?

$3 \div 2 = 1$ (remainder 1)
$7 \div 2 = 3$ (remainder 1)

10 All even numbers, such as 4 and 6, can be divided exactly by two.
True or false?

$6 \div 2 = 3$ $4 \div 2 = 2$

8 All numbers can be divided by 1 and themselves.
True or false?

$6 \div 6 = 1$ $6 \div 1 = 6$

11 Any number that ends in 5 can be divided by 5.
True or false?

$25 \div 5 = 5$
$5 \div 5 = 1$
$105 \div 5 = 21$

12 Multiply a number by one and the answer is always the same as the number you started with.
True or false?

$7 \times 1 = 7$ $4 \times 1 = 4$

9 Multiplications can be done in any order.
True or false?

$2 \times 4 = 8$
$4 \times 2 = 8$

3 False	6 True	9 True	12 True
2 True	5 True	8 True	11 True
1 True	4 True	7 False	10 True

29

Useful words

array
This is an arrangement of objects in rows and columns.

This is an array of marbles.

column
A column is set out down the page.

This is a column.

divide
When you want to find out how many 3s there are in 12, you divide.

This is the division sign.
$$12 \div 3 = 4$$

doubling
Doubling is the same as multiplying by two.

$$5 \times 2 = 10$$

eighth
When you divide a cake into eight equal slices, each slice is an eighth.

This is an eighth.

fraction
This is part of a whole. A piece of cake is a fraction of the whole cake.

This is a fraction.

halving
Halving is the same as dividing by two.

$$14 \div 2 = 7$$

inverse
This means the opposite. The inverse of multiplying by 3 is dividing by 3.

$$2 \times 3 = 6$$
$$6 \div 3 = 2$$

multiply
When you add together the same number again and again, you are multiplying. So 3 + 3 is the same as 2 x 3.

$$3 + 3 = 6$$
$$2 \times 3 = 6$$
This is the multiplication sign.

quarter
When you divide a cake into four equal slices, each slice is a quarter.

This is a quarter.

remainder
The remainder is what is left over when a division cannot be done exactly.

$$7 \div 2 = 3 \text{ (remainder 1)}$$

row
A row is set out across the page.

This is a row.

square array
This type of array has the same number of rows and columns.

times
This means the same as multiply by.

times table
This is a set of multiplications up to 10 or 12 set out on the page.

1 x 4	=	4
2 x 4	=	8
3 x 4	=	12
4 x 4	=	16
5 x 4	=	20
6 x 4	=	24
7 x 4	=	28
8 x 4	=	32
9 x 4	=	36
10 x 4	=	40
11 x 4	=	44
12 x 4	=	48

This is the four times table.

Multiplication square

In this square, there are answers to multiplications up to 12. To use it, multiply a number down one side by a number along the top. Try 4 x 5. Read across and down as shown below. Where do the numbers meet? The answer is 20, so 4 x 5 = 20. Now try the other multiplications in the square.

Multiply using these numbers.

1	2	3	4	5	6	7	8	9	10	11	12
2	4	6	8	10	12	14	16	18	20	22	24
3	6	9	12	15	18	21	24	27	30	33	36
4	8	12	16	20	24	28	32	36	40	44	48
5	10	15	20	25	30	35	40	45	50	55	60
6	12	18	24	30	36	42	48	54	60	66	72
7	14	21	28	35	42	49	56	63	70	77	84
8	16	24	32	40	48	56	64	72	80	88	96
9	18	27	36	45	54	63	72	81	90	99	108
10	20	30	40	50	60	70	80	90	100	110	120
11	22	33	44	55	66	77	88	99	110	121	132
12	24	36	48	60	72	84	96	108	120	132	144

Multiply using these numbers.

Index

Notes for parents and teachers

This book helps children to become confident with the essential mathematical skills of multiplying and dividing. These are calculations that children use every day, such as how much do several packets of sweets cost or are there enough sweets to share with friends? Throughout the book, children pick up basic skills and on this page, there are other ideas for them to try.

Basic building blocks

Children may chant for their favourite football team, 2, 4, 6, 8... or count their pocket money. When they do, they are using multiplication patterns. Encourage children to use these basic building blocks, which are learned usually through repetition.

● Share out the apples from pages 10 and 11. How many multiplication patterns can children make? Now ask them what's the longest pattern they can make.

Times tables

Tables are a way of setting out information clearly. When multiplications are set out in tables, patterns in the answers are easy to see and memorise. The answers in the ten times table, for example, always end in zero.

● Encourage children to make a wall chart of the multiplication square on page 31. Then quiz the kids. What's 5 × 3 or 6 × 2?

Sharing things out

There are two important ideas to work with when you think about sharing. The first is the size of each share, and the second is the number of shares. You also need to look at what's left over, the remainder.

● Ask children what's biggest, $\frac{1}{2}$, $\frac{1}{4}$ or $\frac{1}{8}$. Use the cake slices on pages 20 and 21 to show them why. Then try other fractions. Is $\frac{1}{12}$ bigger than $\frac{1}{6}$?

● Practise sharing with the bug cards from pages 8 and 9. If the cards are put into piles of two, how many people can have a pile? How many are left over if you put the cards into piles of 3 or 7? Share out the cards to show the answers.

Following the rules

There's one important rule used in maths that relates to the order in which calculations are done. Division can only be done in a set order. However, multiplication can be done in any order, so 3 × 4 has the same answer as 4 × 3.

● Look at the five and ten times tables on page 12. Ask children to tell you another way to multiply 2 × 5 or 6 × 10 to reach the same answer.

Make it fun!

Encourage children to enjoy maths by praising their efforts to learn. Give them fun quizzes – always finish on a correct answer to keep their attitudes positive and their confidence levels high.